INTERACT with a
**GIANT JAPANESE
SPIDER CRAB!**

DESCEND IN a
deep-sea
submersible and
**EXPLORE THE
OCEAN DEPTHS**

Come face to face with a
lifesize **GREAT WHITE SHARK!**

Take a closer look
at whales, sharks, rays
and other amazing
sea creatures!

Credits

The publishers would like to thank the following sources for their kind permission to reproduce the pictures in this book.

PICTURE CREDITS

2-3, 4-5 Shutterstock.com, 6 (bottom left) Clouds Hill Imaging Ltd/Corbis, 6-7 Denis Scott/Corbis, 7 & 8 (centre left) iStockphoto.com, 8 (bottom left) Jeff Foot/Getty Images, 8 (bottom centre) Mike Theiss/Ultimate Chase/Corbis, 8-9 Oceans Image/Photoshot, 9 iStockphoto.com, 10-11 Simon Margetson Travel/Alamy Stock Photo, 11 (left) NHPA/Photoshot, 11 (top) Sabena Jane Blackbird/ Alamy Stock Photo, 12 Shutterstock.com, 12-13 & 13 (left) Oceans-Image/Photoshot, 13 (right) National Geographic Creative/Getty Images, 14 (bottom centre) Steven Kazlowski/naturepl.com, 14 (bottom right) Doc White/naturepl.com, 14-15 Denis Scott/Corbis, 15 (top) Mark Carwardine/ naturepl.com, 16 (bottom left) iStockphoto.com, 16 (centre) Tim Graham/Getty Images, 16-17 Gary Bell/Getty Images, 17 (top) Oceans-Image/Photoshot, 17 (bottom) Jurgen Freund/naturepl. com, 18 (bottom left & centre) NHPA/Photoshot, 18-19 Andy Rouse/naturepl.com, 20 (bottom left) NHPA/Photoshot, 20 (bottom centre) Rod Williams/naturepl.com, 22 (left) Doc White/naturepl. com, 22 (bottom centre) & 22-23 Oceans-Image/Photoshot , 23 (top) David Fleetham/naturepl. com, 23 (bottom) Justin Lewis/Getty Images, 24 & 25 (bottom right) Seapics.com, 25 (bottom centre) Ministry of Fisheries via Getty Images, 26 (bottom) iStockphoto.com, 26 (top) Bob Thomas/Popperfoto/Getty Images, 26-27 Denis Scott/Corbis, 28, 29 (bottom left), 29 (bottom right) Norbert Wu/Minden Pictures/FLPA, 29 (bottom centre) Doc White/naturepl.com, 30 Corbis, 31 (top) Peter Arnold, Inc./Alamy, 31 (right) Emory Kristof/National Geographic/Getty Images

Every effort has been made to acknowledge correctly and contact the source and/or copyright holder of each picture and Carlton Books Limited apologises for any unintentional errors or omissions, which will be corrected in future editions of this book.

THIS IS A CARLTON BOOK

Text, design and illustration copyright
© Carlton Books Limited 2016

Published in 2016 by Carlton Books Limited
An imprint of the Carlton Publishing Group
20 Mortimer Street, London W1T 3JW

A catalogue record for this book is available from the British Library.

ISBN: 978-1-78312-233-2
Printed in Dongguan, China

Executive editor: Selina Wood
Design manager: Emily Clarke
Design: WildPixel Ltd.
Cover design: WildPixel Ltd.
Illustrators: Ryan Forshaw, Mark Walker
Picture research: Steve Behan
Production: Charlotte Larcombe

OCEAN MONSTERS

Nicola Davies

Interactive | Sea Tour

Enter the submersible!

Get set to dive deep on your watery world tour! Descend in the deep-sea submersible and discover spectacular fish, amazing whales and scary sharks!

Need some help? Check out our useful website for helpful tips and problem-solving advice:

www.icarlton.co.uk/help

Great White
Shark

Three words that make most people shiver, the great white shark has the worst reputation of any marine creature, and has been labelled as a man eater…

STRIKING SWIMMER

Always super-speedy, the great white shark strikes from below. It stalks the murky depths in silence, looking up at the surface to spot the silhouette of potential prey … then it shoots up to attack.

This shark's first bite is often to test if the victim is worth eating. Nice plump seals are a favourite on the menu and are eaten in a few bites; smaller prey may be swallowed whole. But human swimmers and surfers are usually too skinny and bony to pass the test, and after one or two bites the shark spits them out. Unfortunately, even being nibbled by a 5-metre-long great white can kill you.

LEFT: *The shark's tiny tooth-like scales (magnified here) are known as dermal dentricals and help it to move through the water without a sound.*

BIG, BRUTAL BITES

A shark is never without its bite. Its teeth are arranged in rows, one behind the other, so that if a tooth is lost it is replaced immediately by another. Sharks get through thousands of them in a lifetime, which is why so many fossils of their teeth have been found.

A great white's teeth are sharp, very pointed, and triangular in shape to give them strength. They also get broader with age. Young great whites have skinny, isosceles triangle-shaped teeth – good for grabbing small, slippery prey and swallowing them whole. The adults have squat, equilateral triangle-shaped teeth with enough strength to slice through the flesh and bone of seals and other big mammals.

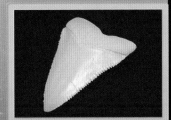

RIGHT: *The teeth of the great white shark have sharp, serrated edges, like a steak knife.*

Interactive **Sea Tour**

Meet a lifesize Great White Shark!
Take a deep breath, make this Great White Shark lifesize and see how big it really is!

KILLER SENSES

Three main senses help the great white to track down its prey…

Smell

A shark's nose is so sensitive it could detect a drop of blood in a swimming pool. The difference in smell strength between its left and right nostrils helps it to tell where a scent comes from. A series of tiny pores along the shark's body, called the lateral line, picks up the slightest ripple in the water. This information might tell the shark where a scent-bearing current is coming from, or if prey is moving nearby.

Sight

Sharks can see in bright or dim light by changing the size of the pupils that let light into their eyes. In low light their sight is ten times better than ours. Movements that might look blurred to humans are sharp to the great white's eye, which would notice each of the 25 individual pictures that make up one second of a film.

Electrical sense

All living creatures have nerves, which work by sending electrical messages. Sharks use this electricity to find prey hidden in the darkness. Gel-filled pits on the great white's snout can sense the tiny electrical charges of nearby living creatures, and even the magnetic fields of rocks on which seals and other prey might be resting.

SIZE

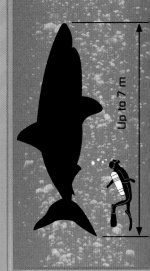

Up to 7 m

DEPTH (M)

0

100

200

300

400

500

Often near the surface but regularly dive down to 300 m

LOCATION

Almost everywhere where the sea is warmer than 12 °C

Killer Whale

Like black-and-white torpedos, killer whales slice through the waves. Also known as orcas, they are the wolves of the sea, taking any prey they choose – even whales twice their size.

ABOVE: *Dorsal fins can be 2 m high on the biggest male killer whales.*

TOP SPEED

A killer whale is easy to spot at sea, with its striking black-and-white pattern and a black dorsal fin rising up from its back. It moves fast, cruising for hours at around 10 km/h or putting on short bursts of speed of up to 48 km/h! Pretty impressive for an animal that can be up to 8 m long and weigh 5 tonnes.

We are family

Killer-whale babies, or "calves", usually stay with their pod for their whole lives, which can be 50 to 100 years. They learn the special hunting techniques of their pod from the adults around them. Different pods sometimes get together – perhaps teaming up for a special hunt, or mingling just to socialize. This gives killer whales the chance to find a mate outside of their own family.

Captive killers

You may have seen killer whales in captivity performing spectacular tricks. But many have been taken from their families in the wild. They might seem quite well and may even breed, but for animals used to roaming the open sea, even the biggest tank is simply a prison.

TEAM WORK

Size, strength and speed help to make killer whales top predators, but the other key to their success is team work. They live in family groups called pods and work together to hunt their prey. Each pod knows exactly where and when to catch its chosen victims, and the best way to cooperate to make the hunt a success.

Some pods hunt by herding shoals of fish, while others ride waves onto beaches to grab seal pups. There are also those that chase whales over huge distances until they are too tired to protect themselves.

ABOVE: *Killer whales live and hunt together in family groups called pods.*

Interactive **Sea Tour**

360° Killer Whale
Take a closer look at this formidable hunter with its striking markings and large dorsal fin!

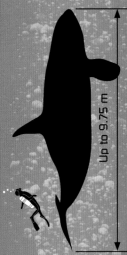

SIZE

Up to 9.75 m

DEPTH (M)

0

100

200

300

400

500

Can dive down to lower depths

LOCATION

All the oceans of the world

Giant Japanese Spider Crab

Meet a crab with fearsome pincers and legs so long it could cuddle a small car! No wonder there are stories of it feasting on the bodies of drowned sailors...

BIG... BIGGER...

The biggest giant Japanese spider crab on record measured 3.7 m from tip to tip of its longest, pincer-carrying forelegs. At 18.5 kg, it weighed about the same as a collie dog! But as with all deep-sea monsters, there are many stories of even bigger spider crabs...

In 1921, fishermen from Honshu, Japan, claimed they caught a crab with a 5.8-metre leg span. And back in 1886, European visitors to a Japanese fishing village say that they saw 3-metre-long spider-crab legs that were propped up outside a fisherman's hut. If their story was true, those legs belonged to a crab with a leg span of 6.7 m – big enough to give a small truck a hug!

BIGGEST?

So could there be even bigger crabs lurking down in the depths with 20-metre leg spans and bodies weighing 100 kg? The answer is almost certainly "no" because of the way spider-crab bodies are put together.

Crabs belong to a group of animals called arthropods, which also includes insects and spiders. Arthropods have jointed legs, a bit like drinking straws joined together with elastic bands. These work well for small creatures but not for big ones. A 100 kg spider crab simply wouldn't be able to walk with such spindly legs and weak joints. But even at 3.7 m, Japanese spider crabs are still the biggest arthropods on Earth. Watch out for them if you ever go diving off the coast of Japan!

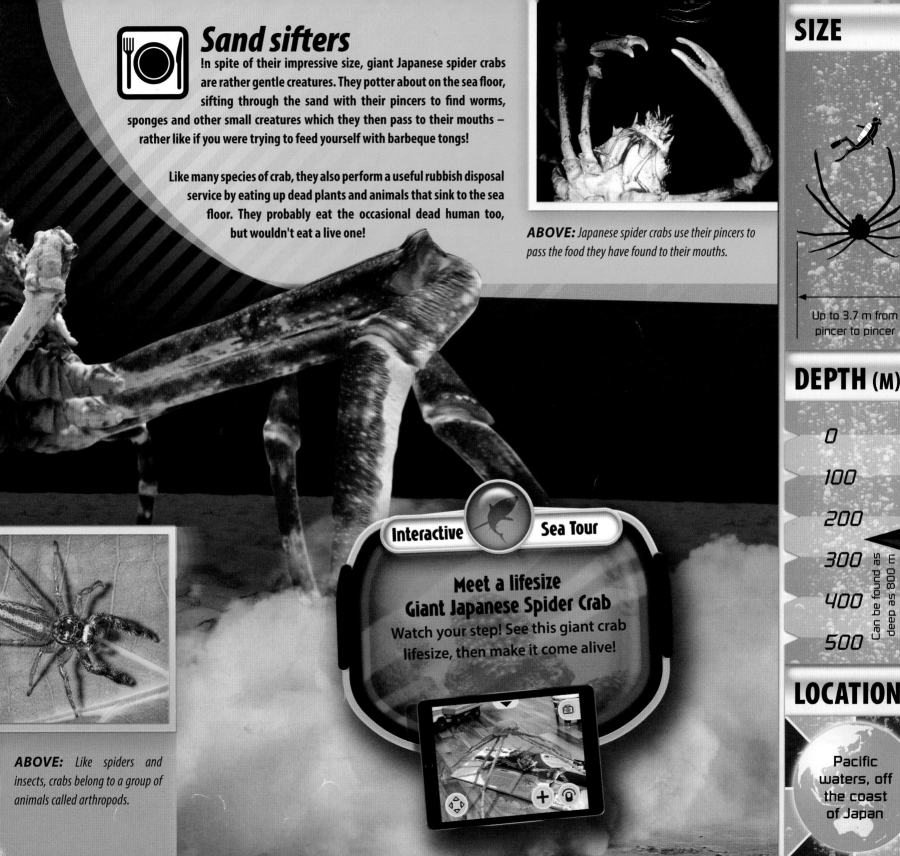

Sand sifters

In spite of their impressive size, giant Japanese spider crabs are rather gentle creatures. They potter about on the sea floor, sifting through the sand with their pincers to find worms, sponges and other small creatures which they then pass to their mouths – rather like if you were trying to feed yourself with barbeque tongs!

Like many species of crab, they also perform a useful rubbish disposal service by eating up dead plants and animals that sink to the sea floor. They probably eat the occasional dead human too, but wouldn't eat a live one!

ABOVE: *Japanese spider crabs use their pincers to pass the food they have found to their mouths.*

ABOVE: *Like spiders and insects, crabs belong to a group of animals called arthropods.*

Interactive **Sea Tour**

Meet a lifesize Giant Japanese Spider Crab
Watch your step! See this giant crab lifesize, then make it come alive!

SIZE

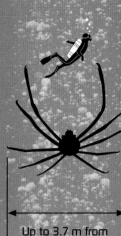

Up to 3.7 m from pincer to pincer

DEPTH (M)

0

100

200

300

400

500

Can be found as deep as 800 m

LOCATION

Pacific waters, off the coast of Japan

Ocean Sunfish

With a body like a fallen moon and a strange frill where a proper fishy tail should be, the ocean sunfish is not only peculiar – it's a giant too!

HEAVY-GOING

A normal-sized adult sunfish, or "mola mola", is huge. Weighing around a tonne, it's about 1.8 m in length and 2.4 m from fin-tip to fin-tip. But the biggest sunfish can be much, much larger…

In 1908 the *SS Fiona's* propeller struck a sunfish outside Sydney harbour, Australia. When the great creature was disentangled, it was found to be 3.1 m long and to weigh 2.23 tonnes! This makes the ocean sunfish the heaviest bony fish in the sea (unlike sharks and rays whose skeletons are made of cartilage).

ABOVE: *A sunfish bathes in the sun's rays to warm up its body after a dive into the cold depths.*

SLOW AND STEADY

Ocean sunfish are great travellers, crossing thousands of kilometres of ocean. It's hard to imagine how such a big round body can swim with just two little fins. They are rather slow but keep up a steady pace and can cover 26 km in a day.

Whenever sunfish dive down through cold waters in search of food, they need to warm up afterwards. They do this by sunbathing at the surface – a behaviour that has earned them their English name.

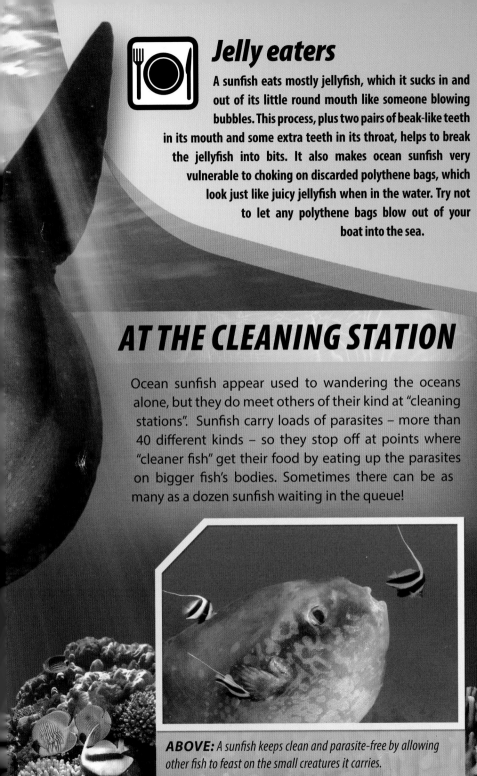

Jelly eaters

A sunfish eats mostly jellyfish, which it sucks in and out of its little round mouth like someone blowing bubbles. This process, plus two pairs of beak-like teeth in its mouth and some extra teeth in its throat, helps to break the jellyfish into bits. It also makes ocean sunfish very vulnerable to choking on discarded polythene bags, which look just like juicy jellyfish when in the water. Try not to let any polythene bags blow out of your boat into the sea.

AT THE CLEANING STATION

Ocean sunfish appear used to wandering the oceans alone, but they do meet others of their kind at "cleaning stations". Sunfish carry loads of parasites – more than 40 different kinds – so they stop off at points where "cleaner fish" get their food by eating up the parasites on bigger fish's bodies. Sometimes there can be as many as a dozen sunfish waiting in the queue!

ABOVE: *A sunfish keeps clean and parasite-free by allowing other fish to feast on the small creatures it carries.*

So many babies!

Adult sunfish have rubbery skin, thick enough to stop a bullet. But their babies are not so tough and many end up as dinner before they reach adulthood. This could be why ocean sunfish females lay 300 million eggs in one go!

Baby sunfish look like nine-pointed stars and grow really fast, increasing their weight a whopping 60 million times before reaching adulthood. That's like a tadpole growing into a frog the size of a truck!

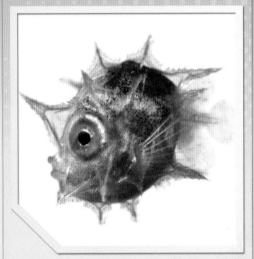

ABOVE: *A baby sunfish is star-shaped and very vulnerable to predators that might eat it, despite the many spines covering its body.*

SIZE

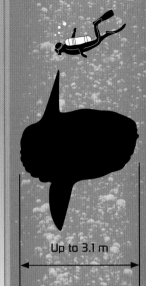

Up to 3.1 m

DEPTH (M)

0

100

200

300

400

500

Usually near the surface but can dive down to 200 m

LOCATION

All tropical and temperate oceans in waters warmer than 12 °C

Blue Whale

A blue whale is as long as three buses, and weighs the same as 83 great white sharks! Everything about this creature is truly monster-sized...

Noisy neighbours

Blue whales are often alone when you see them in the ocean, but this doesn't mean they're lonely. They keep in touch with each other by making a variety of deep moaning and humming sounds, some far too low for human ears to hear easily. These sounds can be incredibly loud – louder even than a jet aircraft taking off – and have been shown to travel through hundreds of kilometres of sea.

BIG-HEARTED

When you see a blue whale in the ocean, its long back seems to go on for ever! At around 30 m long, it's the biggest animal ever to have lived on Earth. Nearly twice as heavy as the largest dinosaur known to man, this creature needs a heart the size of a small car to keep it alive.

This huge heart pumps ten tonnes of blood through a million kilometres of blood vessels, some of them big enough for you to swim down. Even so, it beats very slowly – just 5 or 6 times in a single minute.

RIGHT: *The pleated throat of the blue whale expands to take in millions of krill in one great gulp.*

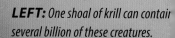

LEFT: *One shoal of krill can contain several billion of these creatures.*

Monster baby

A newborn blue whale, or "calf", is 7.5 m in length – that's even longer than an SUV! But it doesn't stay this size for long… Drinking 500 litres a day of Mum's milk, richer than double cream, makes the blue whale calf grow by 4 kg every hour! By the time the calf is 6 months old, it is 17 tonnes heavier than when it was born, and nearly twice as long.

TINY FOOD

Blue whales may be enormous but their food is teeny. They feed on krill – shrimp-like creatures about the size of your little finger. It takes a lot of shrimp to feed a blue whale, and luckily krill swarm together in their billions. Pleats in the blue whale's throat open out when it feeds, allowing it to swallow a whole shoal of krill in one huge gulp.

The whale then sieves the krill from the water using its baleen plates. Each plate is like a giant, bristly dagger, and hundreds of them grow, one behind the other, from the whale's upper jaw. Their overlapping bristles allow the gulped water to flow back out but trap the krill inside the whale.

Interactive   **Sea Tour**

360° Blue Whale
Take a closer look at this remarkable gentle giant!

SIZE

Up to 33 m

DEPTH (M)

0

100

200

300

400

500

Can dive down to 500 m

LOCATION

All the oceans of the world

Box Jellyfish

There are killers in the beautiful, blue waters of the Australian Barrier Reef. Some box jellyfish are as big as a hat, some are smaller than a fingertip, but all have stings that can kill a human in minutes...

DEADLY TO HUMANS

Humans aren't on the box jellyfish menu – at least not yet – but the touch of a single tentacle can be enough to kill a man. The cocktail of poisons in a box-jelly sting causes muscle cramps, damages nerves and eats through skin, leading to terrible pain, paralysis and heart failure in humans.

Some victims die of shock or drowning before they even reach the shore. This has led scientists to believe that many deaths previously though to have been caused by drowning or heart attacks were in fact the result of deadly box-jelly encounters.

LEFT: *A seaside sign warns bathers of the risk of box jellyfish stings. Don't swim where you see this sign!*

SUPER-FAST KILLERS

Box jellies aren't really jellyfish, and are only relatives of the animals we usually call by that name. Real jellyfish are slow moving creatures that drift with the waves, but box jellies are fast swimming, active predators.

Though fragile as wet tissue-paper, box jellyfish are the deadliest creatures in the sea, each with up to 60 stinging tentacles and a big appetite. They eat fish, and, to avoid having their delicate bodies ripped apart by the struggles of their prey, their stings must kill super-fast. Each tentacle can carry 30,000 stinging cells, which fire like arrows and inject enough lethal poison to kill fish instantly.

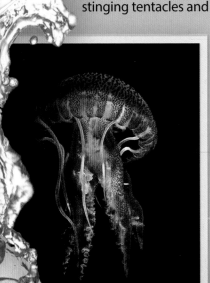

LEFT: *A real jellyfish like this one moves slowly and is only a relative of the fast-swimming box jellyfish.*

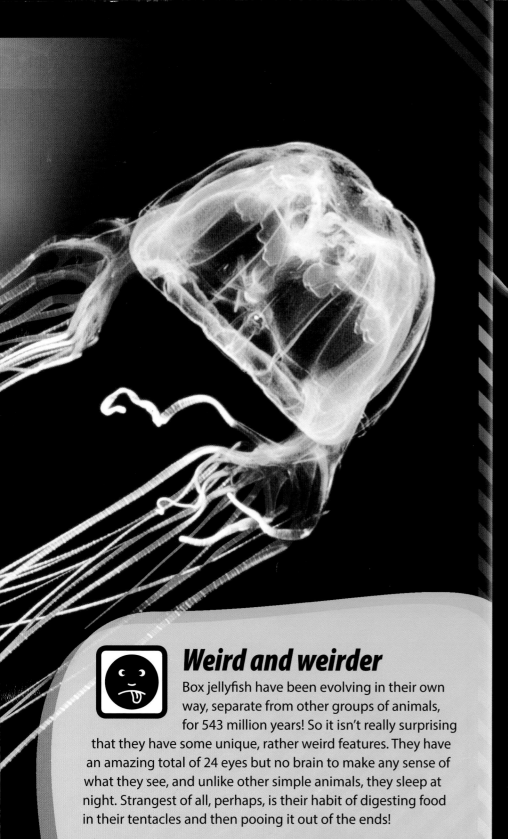

Survivors' secrets

There's one animal on which box jellyfish have no effect at all. Sea turtles eat box jellies as part of their diet but aren't harmed by their stings. The reason is a mystery, but in the future we may learn the turtles' secret and swim without fear.

Coming soon to a sea near you…

There are 36 different kinds of box jellyfish, with scientists discovering new species every year. The biggest and most deadly is the hat-sized "sea wasp", which has 3-metre-long tentacles. But smaller peanut-sized species can cause Irukandji syndrome – intense pain and raised blood pressure that can put victims in hospital or even be fatal.

Box jellies appear to be spreading. No longer found only in the tropical waters of the Pacific and Indian oceans, they are now showing up in parts of the Atlantic and Mediterranean too. There's no antidote to box jellyfish stings but vinegar can stop any untriggered stinging cells from firing.

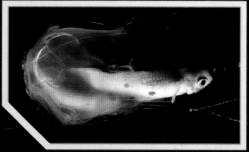

ABOVE: *A peanut-sized box jellyfish attacks a tiny fish.*

Weird and weirder

Box jellyfish have been evolving in their own way, separate from other groups of animals, for 543 million years! So it isn't really surprising that they have some unique, rather weird features. They have an amazing total of 24 eyes but no brain to make any sense of what they see, and unlike other simple animals, they sleep at night. Strangest of all, perhaps, is their habit of digesting food in their tentacles and then pooing it out of the ends!

SIZE

Up to 3.2 m

DEPTH (M)

0

100

200

300

400

500

Found in shallow coastal waters

LOCATION

Mainly the Pacific and Indian Oceans, but spreading

Whale Shark

Imagine a shark as long as a bus swimming towards you, with a mouth wide enough to swallow a sofa. It's a whale shark – but you're much too big to be its dinner!

SOUP SIEVERS

If you are giant-sized, you need a giant amount of food. So whale sharks, like many of the sea's largest creatures, eat huge portions of a food that's small but very plentiful: plankton.

Plankton is like a soup of plants and animals, and to get the bits from this soup whale sharks have a filter system. Sieves made of skin line their throats and gills and, when a whale shark sucks in water, these sieves hold onto anything bigger than a pinhead. Whale sharks can eat small fish too, if they are nicely bunched together in a shoal and easy to gulp!

BELOW: *Plankton are microscopic plants and animals that live in the oceans of the world.*

Sharks in the soup

All over the world, all types of shark are under threat from humans who kill them and use them to make soup, polish, food, leather, lipsticks, petfood and even souvenirs. But surely a beautiful, gentle giant like the whale shark is worth more to us alive, than dead and made into soup? Try to make sure nothing you eat or use has got shark in it!

MYSTERIOUS WANDERERS

Whale sharks must wander to find their food, sometimes travelling thousands of kilometers in a year. Where plankton is plentiful, many whale sharks will gather to feed, but when the plankton bloom is over, the whale sharks disappear. In spite of their size, they are very mysterious animals that we don't know much about. For instance, although we know they give birth to live babies, we we can only guess where in the world this happens!

Interactive **Sea Tour**

360° Whale Shark
Take a closer look at this mysterious shark with its large mouth and beautiful markings.

SIZE

Up to 12.5 m

DEPTH (M)

0

100

200

300

400

500

Often near the surface but can dive down to 700 m

LOCATION

All tropical and warm temperate waters

Giant Tube
Worms

2,500 m and more below sea level, water hotter than boiling gushes from splits in the Earth's crust. This is the home of the giant tube worm…

BLACK SMOKERS

At a depth of 2,500 m under the sea, the Earth's crust splits open and forms deep cracks known as hydrothermal vents. Here, the molten heart of the Earth bubbles up and heats water trapped below the seabed. This water then spews out, four times hotter than boiling, but kept from turning into steam by the great weight of seawater above it.

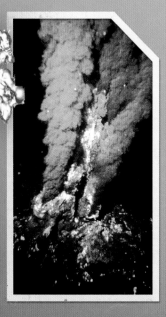

Where this hot water meets the cold water of the deep ocean, towers of black toxic chemicals form, with dark water spouting from their chimney-like tops. These are called black smokers and around them, where the water isn't quite so hot, are colonies of tube worms, like fields of underwater flowers. How can anything live in such a devilishly inhospitable place?

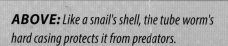

ABOVE: *Like a snail's shell, the tube worm's hard casing protects it from predators.*

MILLIONS OF HELPERS

Each giant tube worm has a long white body with a red plume at its end. It has no eyes, no mouth and no gut. The red pigment in its plume is the same as the one in your blood that carries oxygen around your body. But for the giant tube worm it soaks up chemicals from the hydrothermal vent to feed to billions of bacteria that live inside the worm.

In return for being fed and housed, the bacteria make food for the worm. This kind of relationship where two types of animal both benefit from working together is called "symbiosis". The arrangement works so well that the worms can grow to be 2 m long in just a year and a half.

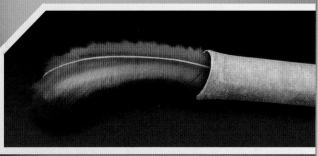

ABOVE: *The red plume at the end of each worm soaks up valuable chemicals from the hydrothermal vent.*

Protective armour

A tube worm's tough tube is made of the same stuff as an insect's armoured skin. When tube worms feel a movement in the water they wiggle inside, like a snail pulling itself inside its shell for protection. But the worms aren't always quick enough to escape the many mouths of those that want to eat them – whole armies of shrimp, crabs and small fish! Far away from our world of sunlight, tube worms are the start of an under-sea food chain.

Endings and beginnings

Hydrothermal vents don't last forever. If the split in the Earth's crust closes over, all the tube worms and the life they support soon die. But somewhere else on the ocean floor another split will open up, and tiny tube worm larvae will take up residence. Unlike the grown-up worms, these larvae have mouths so that they can swallow their friendly bacteria. Then they start to grow, without eating or seeing at all, down there in the dark, dark depths.

SIZE

Up to 2 m

DEPTH (M)

0

500

1,000

1,500

2,000

2,500

2,500 m deep and below

LOCATION

Only in the deepest oceans, around hydrothermal vents

Manta Ray

Swooping over the reef, the manta ray looks like a shadowy creature from another dimension. Sailors once called it the "devil fish" and believed its great dark wings could crush human victims to death...

ABOVE: *In spite of their size, manta rays are agile swimmers. They can even jump right out of the ocean – known as "breaching".*

FIN WINGS

In reality, manta rays are gentle giants, harmless plankton feeders and one of the most graceful creatures of the deep. They are related to sharks, and their huge wings – which can measure 7.6 m from tip to tip – are actually big, flat pectoral fins. Mantas swim by slowly flapping them and can travel hundreds of kilometres in just a few days, to find food, mates or a safe place to breed.

Interactive **Sea Tour**

360° Manta Ray
Take a closer look at this shadowy creature, with its huge wing-like fins.

Mantas in danger

Sharks and killer whales like to make a meal of manta rays, and even large adults carry scars from close shaves! One reason mantas can survive these attacks is that their wounds are attended to by "cleaner fish", who specialize in eating the dead or infected skin – as well as the parasites – of other animals. Mantas cannot survive attacks by humans, however. Thousands are killed every year for their gills, which are used in Chinese medicine, and for their fins, which are used in shark-fin soup as sharks themselves become more and more rare.

EATING AND BREATHING

Two horn-like fins on the manta's head funnel water into its mouth, over its gills and out again through the gill slits on its underside. Like all fish, mantas breathe water through their gills. But manta gills do another job too: they are covered with a sticky, spongy layer that captures tiny sea creatures and fish eggs for the manta to eat. Manta food doesn't need chewing, so this creature's 300 teeth are just tiny pinheads without a real job!

ABOVE: The gill slits of the manta ray filter both oxygen and food from the sea water.

⚡ A sting in the tail

Manta rays are related to stingrays. One way to tell different species of rays apart is by the size and shape of their "sting" – the poisonous spine at the end of their tails. Studying manta ray stings has shown that there are actually two different species of manta. The biggest mantas wander over thousands of kilometres of ocean and still have the remains of a sting – just like their stingray relatives. But the smaller, more home-loving kind of mantas don't have any sting at all.

ABOVE: The stingray is a relative of the much larger manta ray.

Colossal Squid

Very big – and pretty ugly, except to others of its kind – the colossal squid was thought to be just a seafarer's story for most of the 20th century...

REAL OR IMAGINARY?

Just like its slightly smaller cousin, the giant squid, the colossal squid was believed to be an imaginary creature for many decades. The first signs of this monster appeared in 1925 when whalers found two vast tentacles in the stomach of a sperm whale. They were bigger, thicker and nastier than the tentacles of the more familiar giant squid, which at that time was thought to be the biggest squid in the ocean. What could these huge tentacles possibly belong to?

Not until this century have live specimens been found and photographed. In 2003, a colossal squid was caught alive by fishermen in the Antarctic Ocean and brought to New Zealand for scientific analysis. The body of this creature was around 2.5 m long – a monstrous fact in itself. But the scientists concluded that it was a youngster, only two-thirds grown. Had it lived to become an adult, its body would have been 4 m in length!

LEFT: *A scientist examines the sharp hooks on the colossal squid's tentacles, which can swivel to dig into the flesh of victims.*

DEEP-SEA WARS

The colossal squid is a deep pinky-red colour all over. In the depths where it lives red light cannot penetrate, so it looks dark in the blackness. Invisible to its victims, the colossal squid has two extra-long prey-catching tentacles that are covered with needle-sharp hooks. It is big enough and nasty enough to go for really huge fish, like the 2-metre-long, 200-kilogram Patagonian tooth fish.

So how might this giant react to an attack from a sperm whale? We can only guess. But the evidence suggests that it would put up a good fight because some sperm whales carry the scars of those swivelling hooks. The squid probably wouldn't win, however. Squid beaks have been found in large male sperm whale stomachs, and from the size of these we know that there must be squid more colossal than any human has ever seen! With bodies 5 m long and 20 m of tentacle, these ten-armed monsters are down there somewhere, ending up as sperm-whale dinners.

Deep-sea discoveries

Fishermen out on the open ocean sometimes get involved in scientific research. In 2007, the crew of a boat fishing in Antarctic waters pulled up a colossal squid on their fishing line. This monster wouldn't let go of the fish they'd caught, and was scooped up in a net. Stored in the boat's freezer, it was taken back to New Zealand for biologists to measure!

ABOVE: *A colossal squid is pulled aboard a fishing boat in Antarctic waters.*

ABOVE: *Like all other types of squid, the colossal squid has horny jaws that look just like a parrot's beak.*

SIZE

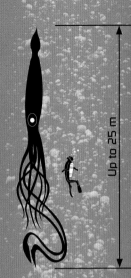

Up to 25 m

DEPTH (M)

0

200

400

600

800

1,00

1,000 m deep and below

LOCATION

Antarctic Ocean

Sperm Whale

A huge triangle-shaped tail disappears beneath the ocean's surface. It's a sperm whale, diving down into the mysterious depths. Listen and you'll hear its clicking sounds...

ABOVE: *Many stories tell of battles between fierce sperm whales and their determined human hunters.*

TICK TOCK

A diving sperm whale sounds rather like a ticking clock. It clicks and listens to the echos to find its way around, just like a killer whale does. Sperm whales are very sociable creatures and also use their clicks for communication with others of their species.

Clicks are so important to the sperm whale that almost all of its huge barrel-shaped head is devoted to making them. The head takes up a third of its body length and is packed full of an oily substance called spermacetti, plus air sacs and tubes. Together, these allow the whale to make its powerful, complicated sounds.

ABOVE: *The sperm whale's huge head makes up one third of its body length.*

BREATH HOLDING

Sperm whales are air-breathing mammals like us, but can dive to depths of 1,000 m, or even 3,000 m, below the surface. They stay down there for up to an hour-and-a-quarter at a time!

Deep breaths at the surface before a dive let the sperm whale store enough oxygen in its blood and muscles for it to hold its breath while it dives – a bit like charging a battery. But when the whale comes up from a long dive, it must rest and recharge its "oxygen battery" before diving again.

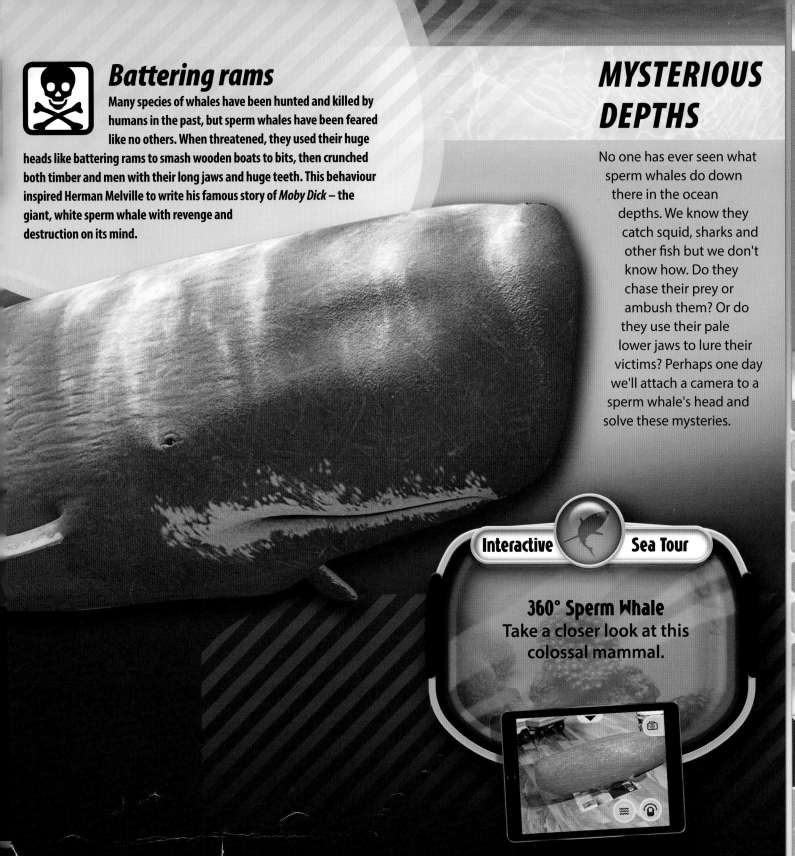

Battering rams

Many species of whales have been hunted and killed by humans in the past, but sperm whales have been feared like no others. When threatened, they used their huge heads like battering rams to smash wooden boats to bits, then crunched both timber and men with their long jaws and huge teeth. This behaviour inspired Herman Melville to write his famous story of *Moby Dick* – the giant, white sperm whale with revenge and destruction on its mind.

MYSTERIOUS DEPTHS

No one has ever seen what sperm whales do down there in the ocean depths. We know they catch squid, sharks and other fish but we don't know how. Do they chase their prey or ambush them? Or do they use their pale lower jaws to lure their victims? Perhaps one day we'll attach a camera to a sperm whale's head and solve these mysteries.

Interactive **Sea Tour**

360° Sperm Whale
Take a closer look at this colossal mammal.

SIZE

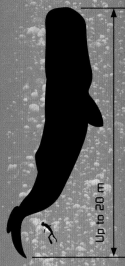

Up to 20 m

DEPTH (M)

0

500

1,000

1,500

2,000

2,500

Can dive down as deep as 3,000 m

LOCATION

All tropical and temperate oceans. Mature males have even been seen near polar ice.

Blackdevil Angler Fish

A thousand metres below the surface of the sea, where it's darker than the deepest cave, lurks a creature straight from your nightmares – the blackdevil angler fish…

BEAUTIFULLY UGLY

The blackdevil angler fish's bulbous body hangs motionless in the water, its huge mouth gaping wide and studded with needle-like teeth. A structure like a tiny fishing rod pokes from its head, luring prey by casting a sickly, greenish glow. Thank goodness this fish isn't monster-sized, being no bigger than a tennis ball!

It may not be beautiful, but the angler fish is very well suited to its home. Down there in the depths of the ocean, food is in short supply and this creature must be ready to swallow whatever prey it can get. Its huge mouth and stomach can stretch enough to allow it to eat victims twice its own size!

HIDDEN HORRORS

Camouflage is important to the blackdevil angler fish. It has red skin that looks soot-black in deep water where there's no light. The only visible part is its little "fishing rod", a sort of skinny fin. At the end of the rod is a small pocket holding a colony of microbes, whose bodies glow with a greenish light. The microbes get a safe home in this little pocket and, in return, the angler fish gets a glowing lure – another example of symbiosis.

But there are other, smaller, deep-sea creatures that glow in the dark with a similar greeny light (a quality known as "bioluminescence"). Hungry predators come close to the angler fish's lure, mistaking it for easy prey – and instead end up as its dinner!

Frankenstein's fish

Male angler fish are smaller than your little finger and instead of finding food, they concentrate on finding a female. They pick up the tiniest trace of her scent in the water, and when they find her they bite her side and join with her skin. Pretty soon all that's left of the male is a little tail sticking out of the female's side. But this way neither will need to look for a mate when they want to make angler-fish babies.

LEFT: *The tiny male angler fish fuses with the body of the larger female.*

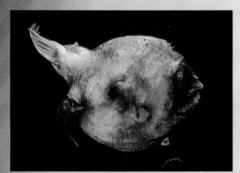

Other deep-sea nightmares

Down there in the depths are many other creatures with faces not even their own mums could love! Try the triple wart sea devil, the female of which can weigh 10 kg, dwarfing the tiny 150 g males. Or take a look at the umbrella mouth gulper, which lives over 2,000 m below the surface. All we know about many of these deep-sea monsters is what they look like. What they eat, how they breed and how long they live are mysteries, waiting for someone like you to answer them…

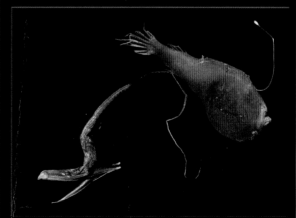

ABOVE: *The umbrella mouth gulper (left) and the triple wart sea devil, another kind of angler fish (right).*

SIZE

Up to 10 cm

DEPTH (M)

0

200

400

600

800

1,000

Sometimes found in shallow water but prefers depths below 1,000 m

LOCATION

All the oceans of the world

Oarfish

For thousands of years, sailors have told tales of sea serpents with huge snake-like bodies and crested heads. But there is a real, live creature behind the legends – the oarfish...

SEA SERPENT

It may not be as powerful as Payanak, a sea serpent said to protect the country of Laos from enemies, but the oarfish is certainly the longest bony fish in the oceans. Its body is like a giant, silvery ribbon and can grow to 15.2 m in length.

It's not only the oarfish's length and snake-like shape that tie in with descriptions of sea serpents. It has a bright red fin stretching the length of its back, a splendid crest on its head, and long red fins to either side. These striking features may have lead to tales of crested and maned sea monsters, and certainly earned the oarfish the name "king of the herrings".

ABOVE: *Could it be that the oarfish lies behind the many legends that exist about sea-serpents?*

ABOVE: *Oarfish are known to hang motionless in the water.*

Interactive — **Sea Tour**

360° Oarfish
Take a closer look at this ribbon-shaped super serpent.